MARTA BREEN

MARTA BREEN (BORN 1976) IS AN AWARD-WINNING NORWEGIAN NON-FICTION WRITER AND JOURNALIST WHO HAS WRITTEN 12 BOOKS ON TOPICS INCLUDING MUSIC, POLITICS, AND WOMEN'S HISTORY. MARTA AND JENNY'S PREVIOUS GRAPHIC NOVEL, *WOMEN IN BATTLE* (2018), HAS BEEN TRANSLATED INTO MORE THAN 20 LANGUAGES. MARTA HAS LECTURED ABOUT FEMINISM AND EQUALITY IN MANY COUNTRIES AROUND THE WORLD.

JENNY JORDAHL

JENNY JORDAHL (BORN 1989) IS AN AWARD-WINNING NORWEGIAN ILLUSTRATOR, GRAPHIC NOVELIST, AND GRAPHIC DESIGNER. SHE DEBUTED AS AN AUTHOR IN 2017 WITH THE CHILDREN'S BOOK *HANNEMONE AND HULDA,* AND HAS ILLUSTRATED NUMEROUS BOOKS IN THE PAST FIVE YEARS. IN 2020, JENNY RECEIVED THE BRAGE PRIZE FOR HER YOUNG ADULT GRAPHIC NOVEL *WHAT HAPPENED TO YOU?*

SMASH THE PATRIARCHY

BY

MARTA BREEN AND JENNY JORDAHL

TRANSLATED FROM NORWEGIAN BY
SIÂN MACKIE

WHERE MEN HAVE *MORE* POWER...

EARN *MORE* MONEY...

AND ARE CONSIDERED SOMEWHAT *MORE* IMPORTANT THAN WOMEN.

BUT HOW DID THIS HAPPEN?

IT'S DIFFICULT TO PINPOINT THE ORIGINS OF THE PATRIARCHY, BUT LET'S START WHERE SO MUCH WESTERN HISTORY BEGINS: ANCIENT GREECE.

ARISTOTLE

PLATO

MANY ANCIENT PHILOSOPHERS WERE INTERESTED IN HOW THE RELATIONSHIP BETWEEN WOMEN AND MEN SHOULD BE ORGANIZED.

PLATO AND HIS STUDENT, ARISTOTLE, DID NOT AGREE AT ALL.

WOMEN AND MEN ARE QUITE ALIKE AND CAN THEREFORE PERFORM SIMILAR TASKS.

IF A WOMAN DEMONSTRATES THAT SHE CAN GOVERN A SOCIETY, THEN LET HER DO SO.

IF A MAN DEMONSTRATES THAT ALL HE CAN DO IS WASH DISHES, THEN LET HIM DO SO.

A STATE THAT ONLY EDUCATES MEN IS LIKE A BODY THAT ONLY EXERCISES ONE ARM.

IF A WOMAN IS THE HEAD OF GOVERNMENT, THEN THE COUNTRY IS IN JEOPARDY.
SILENCE IS AN ORNAMENT FOR WOMEN.
THEY ACT ON ARBITRARY INCLINATIONS AND OPINIONS.
SOPHOCLES, GREECE (CA. 496-406 BCE)
GOING TO SEE A WOMAN? DON'T FORGET THE WHIP!
GEORG WILHELM FRIEDRICH HEGEL, GERMANY (1770-1831)
FRIEDRICH NIETZSCHE, GERMANY (1844-1900)
BOTH JEWS AND WOMEN LACK PERSONALITY.
SEX & CHARACTER
OTTO WEININGER, AUSTRIA (1880-1903)

THE IDEA OF FUNDAMENTAL DIFFERENCES BETWEEN THE SEXES RESULTED IN GIRLS AND BOYS BEING BROUGHT UP VERY DIFFERENTLY.

FOR CENTURIES, IT WAS COMMON FOR BOYS TO RECEIVE THEORETICAL EDUCATION,

BECAUSE THEY WERE SEEN AS LOGICAL AND RATIONAL.

GIRLS WERE TAUGHT TO LOOK AFTER THE HOUSEHOLD AND CHILDREN,

BECAUSE THEY WERE SEEN AS CARING AND EMOTIONAL.

IF SOMEONE IS TO BE ABLE TO THINK BIG THOUGHTS,

OR CREATE GREAT ART,

THE CONDITIONS MUST BE JUST RIGHT.

EASY ACCESS TO KNOWLEDGE...

AND THE OPPORTUNITY TO DELVE DEEP.

HISTORICALLY, WOMEN WERE RARELY ALLOWED SUCH LUXURIES.

WOMEN NEVER HAVE A HALF-HOUR IN ALL THEIR LIVES THAT THEY CAN CALL THEIR OWN, WITHOUT FEAR OF OFFENDING OR OF HURTING SOMEONE.

FLORENCE NIGHTINGALE, UK (1820-1910)

VIRGINIA WOOLF WROTE A WHOLE BOOK ABOUT THIS IN 1929!

SIGH.

A ROOM OF ONE'S OWN BY VIRGINIA WOOLF

FOR CENTURIES, DOCTORS AND SCIENTISTS CLAIMED THAT TOO MUCH KNOWLEDGE COULD HARM A WOMAN'S HEALTH.

IF TEENAGE GIRLS SPEND TOO MUCH TIME READING AND WRITING, THIS CAN AFFECT THE DEVELOPMENT OF THE OVARIES AND UTERUS.

DEAR ME!

THAT MAKES SENSE!

EDWARD HAMMOND CLARKE, USA (1820-1877)

SHE MIGHT BECOME STERILE!

OR HAVE A NERVOUS BREAKDOWN!

MANY SCIENTISTS STUDIED THE DIFFERENCE IN HUMAN BRAIN SIZES.

IT'S QUITE SIMPLY TOO SMALL TO STUDY!

Also too small

too small

too small

too small

too small

THEODOR VON BISCHOFF, GERMANY (1807-1882)

OTHERS CLAIMED THAT WOMEN WHO READ NOVELS RISKED DISAPPEARING INTO A FANTASY WORLD...

AND FORGETTING THEIR PRIMARY ROLE IN LIFE.

WOMEN SHOULD BE FORBIDDEN FROM LEARNING TO WRITE, AND EVEN TO READ. THEIR THOUGHTS CAN THEREBY BE LIMITED AND FOCUSED ON USEFUL DOMESTIC TASKS, INSPIRING THEIR RESPECT FOR OUR SEX.

NICOLAS RESTIF DE LA BRETONNE, FRANCE (1794-1806)

JEEZ...

BUT DIDN'T WOMEN **PROTEST** ALL OF THIS?

YES, ABSOLUTELY. ALWAYS—AND ALL OVER THE WORLD.

UNFORTUNATELY, MANY DARING AND CREATIVE WOMAN IN HISTORY ARE OVERLOOKED, FORGOTTEN, OR RIDICULED.

FOR CENTURIES IT WAS AN UNWRITTEN RULE THAT WOMEN SHOULD STAY OUT OF PUBLIC LIFE.

RELIGIOUS, POLITICAL, AND SCIENTIFIC TEXTS DECLARED THAT THE HOME AND PRIVATE SPHERE WERE A WOMAN'S NATURAL HABITAT.

THEREFORE, THE FIRST WOMEN TO BE IN THE PUBLIC EYE WERE DEEMED *UNNATURAL*.

THROUGHOUT HISTORY, WOMEN USED VARIOUS STRATEGIES TO MAKE THEIR MARK ON PATRIARCHAL SOCIETY.

WELCOME!

SOME UPPER-CLASS WOMEN STARTED INVITING PEOPLE TO LITERARY AND POLITICAL SALONS, OR GATHERINGS, IN THEIR OWN HOMES.

ONE OF THE MOST RENOWNED SALON HOSTESSES WAS FRENCH-SWISS AUTHOR GERMAINE DE STAËL (1766-1817), ALSO KNOWN AS MADAME DE STAËL OR SIMPLY "THE QUEEN OF PARIS."

HER SALONS OFTEN LASTED UNTIL THE NEXT MORNING.

WHEN SHE WAS 20, SHE MARRIED THE SWEDISH BARON ERIK MAGNUS STAËL VON HOLSTEIN.

JUST A MARRIAGE OF CONVENIENCE!

SHE HAD MANY LOVERS, AND EVENTUALLY HAD FIVE CHILDREN.

MADAME DE STAËL EXCHANGED LETTERS WITH WELL-KNOWN FIGURES, SUCH AS RUSSIAN EMPEROR ALEXANDER I, GERMAN POET JOHANN WOLFGANG VON GOETHE, AND AMERICAN PRESIDENT THOMAS JEFFERSON.

SHE WAS A GREAT ADMIRER OF FRENCH MILITARY COMMANDER NAPOLEON I, AND IN 1797 SHE MET HIM.

HELLO!

GERMANY, BLAH BLAH. ITALY! BLAH BLAH BLAH. LITERATURE MUST BE FREE! BLAH BLAH. HAVE YOU READ GOETHE? BLAH BLAH BLAH.

HE WAS NOT AT ALL INTERESTED IN TAKING POLITICAL ADVICE FROM A WOMAN.

NATURE INTENDED WOMEN TO BE OUR SLAVES. THEY ARE OUR PROPERTY.

THE BOOK WAS INTERPRETED AS A POLITICAL STATEMENT, AND NAPOLEON HAD REACHED HIS LIMIT. HE ORDERED MADAME DE STAËL TO LEAVE THE COUNTRY.

DELPHINE

IN 1802, SHE WROTE THE NOVEL *DELPHINE* ABOUT THE FIRST YEARS OF THE FRENCH REVOLUTION.

FOR YEARS, SHE LIVED IN EXILE IN A PALACE IN SWITZERLAND.

Château de Coppet

BUT SHE CONTINUED TO HOLD SALONS AND WRITE BOOKS.

THESE BOOKS WERE DEEMED "ANTI-FRENCH," AND NAPOLEON DESTROYED THOUSANDS OF THEM.

CORINNE

GERMANY

AFTER NAPOLEON WAS EXILED TO THE ISLAND OF SAINT HELENA, MADAME DE STAËL WAS FINALLY ABLE TO RETURN TO HER BELOVED PARIS.

COME IN!

ANOTHER COMMON STRATEGY WAS TO PUBLISH TEXTS ANONYMOUSLY.

AMERICAN AUTHOR EMILY DICKINSON DID THIS.

ONLY SEVEN OF HER POEMS WERE PUBLISHED WHILE SHE WAS ALIVE—ALL ANONYMOUSLY.

WHEN EMILY DIED, HER FAMILY FOUND ALMOST 2,000 POEMS IN HER BEDROOM.

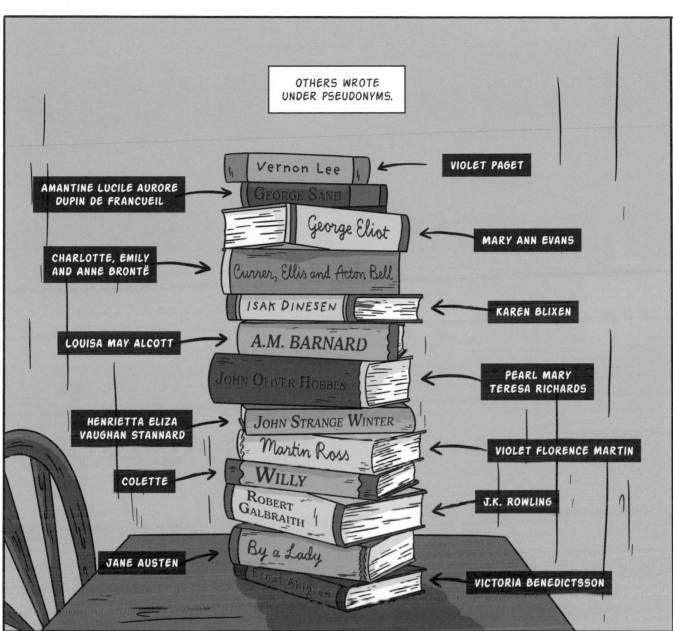

OTHERS WROTE UNDER PSEUDONYMS.

Vernon Lee — VIOLET PAGET

AMANTINE LUCILE AURORE DUPIN DE FRANCUEIL → GEORGE SAND

George Eliot ← MARY ANN EVANS

CHARLOTTE, EMILY AND ANNE BRONTË → Currer, Ellis and Acton Bell

ISAK DINESEN ← KAREN BLIXEN

LOUISA MAY ALCOTT → A.M. BARNARD

JOHN OLIVER HOBBES ← PEARL MARY TERESA RICHARDS

HENRIETTA ELIZA VAUGHAN STANNARD → JOHN STRANGE WINTER

Martin Ross ← VIOLET FLORENCE MARTIN

COLETTE → WILLY

ROBERT GALBRAITH ← J.K. ROWLING

JANE AUSTEN → By a Lady

Ernst Ahlgren ← VICTORIA BENEDICTSSON

SOME ALSO DRESSED AS MEN TO GAIN GREATER FREEDOM.

FRENCH ARMY COMMANDER
JOAN OF ARC (1412-1431)

FRENCH MATHEMATICIAN ÉMILIE
DU CHÂTELET (1706-1749)

FRENCH AUTHOR GEORGE SAND
(1804-1876)

FRENCH ARTIST ROSA
BONHEUR (1822-1899)

SWISS EXPLORER ISABELLE
EBERHARDT (1877-1904)

MEXICAN FREEDOM FIGHTER
PETRA HERRERA (1887-1917)

ONE EARLY ADOPTER OF MALE DISGUISE WAS
PHARAOH HATSHEPSUT (CA. 1508-1458 BCE).

HATSHEPSUT WAS THE DAUGHTER OF THE EGYPTIAN KING THUTMOSE I.

HER FATHER DIED WHEN SHE WAS 12 YEARS OLD.

SHE WAS THEN FORCED TO MARRY HER OWN BROTHER: THUTMOSE II. HE BECAME THE NEW KING.

A FEW YEARS LATER, HE DIED TOO.

SURELY THAT MEANT THAT IT WAS HATSHEPSUT'S TIME TO RULE?

BUT NO, IT WAS THEN DECIDED THAT HER *TWO-YEAR-OLD* NEPHEW WOULD BE EGYPT'S NEW KING.

IT TURNED OUT THAT HER NEPHEW NEEDED HELP TO RULE THE COUNTRY, SO HATSHEPSUT STILL HAD TO STEP IN.

SHE SOON APPOINTED HERSELF PHARAOH OF EGYPT.

SINCE THE ROLE OF PHARAOH WAS NORMALLY RESERVED FOR MEN, SHE DRESSED IN MEN'S CLOTHING AND WORE A FALSE BEARD.

EGYPT BLOSSOMED UNDER HER RULE.

WHILE PREVIOUS RULERS HAD BEEN PREOCCUPIED WITH WAR, HATSHEPSUT WANTED TO BUILD THE COUNTRY'S WEALTH.

SHE SENT A TRADE DELEGATION TO PUNT, A KINGDOM FURTHER SOUTH IN AFRICA. HERE THE EGYPTIANS WERE ABLE TO BUY GOLD, FRANKINCENSE, RESIN, IVORY, AND PERFUME.

RESIN/ KOHL EYELINER.

THE FEMALE KING INITIATED HUNDREDS OF CONSTRUCTION PROJECTS. BEAUTIFUL TEMPLES APPEARED ALL OVER EGYPT.

HATSHEPSUT SERVED AS PHARAOH FOR OVER 20 YEARS.

AFTER SHE DIED, HER NEPHEW—THUTMOSE III—TRIED TO ERADICATE ALL MEMORY OF HER.

LUCKILY, HE WAS UNSUCCESSFUL.

MARRIAGE HAS UNDOUBTEDLY PREVENTED MANY WOMEN FROM PURSUING THEIR DREAMS.

EITHER BECAUSE THEY WERE TOO BUSY WITH ALL THE HOUSEKEEPING...

OR THEIR HUSBANDS FORBID THEM FROM DOING ANYTHING ELSE.

GUSTAV MAHLER (1860-1911)

FROM NOW ON YOU ONLY HAVE ONE JOB: MAKING ME HAPPY! I AM THE COMPOSER, AND YOU ARE MY DEAR SPOUSE AND APPRECIATIVE PARTNER.

YOINK!!

ALMA MAHLER (1879-1964)

HISTORICALLY, MARRIED WOMEN WERE INCAPACITATED.

DO YOU PROMISE TO BE SUBSERVIENT TO YOUR HUSBAND?

AND THEIR NAMES WERE TAKEN FROM THEM.

Mrs. Johnson
~~June Sanger~~
59 Kingsley Road
London

IN PERIODS OF HIGH UNEMPLOYMENT, MARRIED WOMEN WERE FIRED FROM THEIR JOBS.

MANY FEMINISTS VOICED CRITICISM OF MARRIAGE.

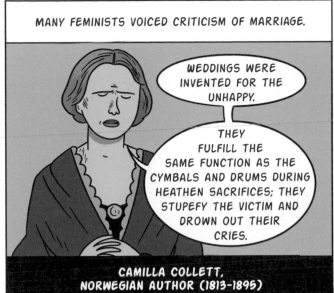

WEDDINGS WERE INVENTED FOR THE UNHAPPY.

THEY FULFILL THE SAME FUNCTION AS THE CYMBALS AND DRUMS DURING HEATHEN SACRIFICES; THEY STUPEFY THE VICTIM AND DROWN OUT THEIR CRIES.

CAMILLA COLLETT, NORWEGIAN AUTHOR (1813-1895)

THE PRINCIPLE OF MARRIAGE IS OBSCENE BECAUSE IT TRANSFORMS AN EXCHANGE THAT SHOULD BE FOUNDED ON A SPONTANEOUS IMPULSE INTO RIGHTS AND DUTIES.

SIMONE DE BEAUVOIR, FRENCH PHILOSOPHER (1908-1986)

THE COMPLETE DESTRUCTION OF TRADITIONAL MARRIAGE AND THE NUCLEAR FAMILY IS THE REVOLUTIONARY OR UTOPIAN GOAL OF FEMINISM.

KATE MILLETT, AMERICAN ACTIVIST (1934-2017)

WHICH CRIME HAS THE FEMALE SEX COMMITTED TO BE SENTENCED TO THE HARSH NECESSITY WHICH CONSISTS OF BEING LOCKED UP ALL HER LIFE EITHER AS A PRISONER OR A SLAVE?

I CALL THE NUNS PRISONERS AND THE MARRIED WOMEN SLAVES.

ONE WOMAN WHO WAS VERY SKEPTICAL OF MARRIAGE WAS QUEEN CHRISTINA OF SWEDEN (1626-1689).

NO!

THE QUEEN WAS VERY WELL READ AND OFTEN INVITED EUROPE'S GREAT THINKERS TO CONVERSE WITH HER AT THE PALACE.

RENÉ DESCARTES (1596-1650)

THE SOUL HAS NO SEX.

SHE STUDIED DAY AND NIGHT, AND MASTERED EIGHT LANGUAGES.

GERMAN
DUTCH
DANISH
FRENCH
ARABIC
HEBREW

CHRISTINA HAD LITTLE INTEREST IN NOBLE REGALIA.

NO!

NO!!

THE PRESSURE TO MARRY FINALLY BECAME TOO MUCH, SO CHRISTINA DECIDED TO GIVE THE THRONE TO HER COUSIN.

NO!!!

SHE MOVED TO ITALY AND BECAME A CATHOLIC.

I LOVE THE STORM AND FEAR THE CALM.

HER INTELLECTUAL ABILITIES—AND LACK OF INTEREST IN MEN—DIDN'T CORRESPOND WITH SOCIETY'S IDEA OF A WOMAN.

CHRISTINA WAS THEREFORE ACCUSED OF BEING A *HERMAPHRODITE.*

AS RECENTLY AS 1965, HER COFFIN WAS OPENED TO INVESTIGATE THIS CLAIM.

HMM...

HMM...

RESEARCHERS CONFIRMED THE QUEEN *WAS A WOMAN.**

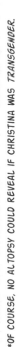

*OF COURSE, NO AUTOPSY COULD REVEAL IF CHRISTINA WAS TRANSGENDER.

46

THE TERM "THE MALE GAZE" WAS COINED BY BRITISH FILM THEORIST LAURA MULVEY IN 1976.

BUT ISN'T THAT NATURAL? WOULDN'T YOU EXPECT MEN TO LOOK AT THE WORLD WITH A MALE GAZE AND WOMEN TO LOOK AT IT WITH A FEMALE GAZE?

YES. BUT THIS ISN'T JUST ABOUT *WHO* IS LOOKING. IT'S ALSO ABOUT *HOW* THEY'RE LOOKING.

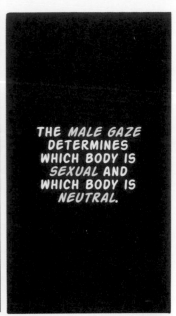

THE *MALE GAZE* DETERMINES WHICH BODY IS *SEXUAL* AND WHICH BODY IS *NEUTRAL.*

HOW ELSE CAN WE EXPLAIN THAT ONLY ONE GENDER IS REQUIRED TO COVER THEMSELVES ACCORDING TO STRICT RULES?

HURRY!

OR APPEARS UNDRESSED ON EVERY OTHER STREET CORNER?

MEN'S NIPPLES ARE NEUTRAL. WOMEN'S NIPPLES ARE SEXUAL.

RAWR!

MEN'S ARMPIT HAIR IS NEUTRAL. WOMEN'S ARMPIT HAIR IS CONTROVERSIAL.

UGH! HORRIBLE!

IN FILMS, THE MALE GAZE IS OFTEN CHARACTERIZED BY HIM PLAYING THE MAIN ROLE, WHILE HER ROLE IS MORE PASSIVE.

WE NEED TO MEET! NOW!

THANKS FOR COMING AT SUCH SHORT NOTICE TO THIS COMPLETELY NORMAL PLACE. SIT!

WHAT'S THIS ABOUT?

FOR EXAMPLE, CONSIDER THE COUNTLESS MOVIE SCENES IN AMERICAN STRIP CLUBS. THE DANCERS DON'T GENERALLY HAVE ANYTHING TO DO WITH THE STORY.

THE CLUB IS JUST A *RANDOM* MEETING PLACE.

DAD'S GOING TO SELL THE COMPANY. TONIGHT!

THAT SNEAK!

THE WOMEN ARE PROPS THAT THE MEN OFTEN IGNORE.

BECAUSE THE STORIES OF THESE WOMEN ARE RARELY TOLD, THE VIEWER ALREADY KNOWS THAT SHE IS UNIMPORTANT TO THE PLOT.

WE NEED TO ACT FAST!

AND THAT'S WHY WE DON'T THINK ABOUT HER EITHER.

SEE YOU TOMORROW!

BYE!

WE DON'T CARE WHERE SHE LIVES OR WHAT SHE DOES WHEN SHE ISN'T WORKING.

HOME

49

THE PROTAGONIST:

SUPPORTING ROLE:

INCIDENTALLY, THE CONCEPT OF VIRGINITY IS ONE OF THE PATRIARCHY'S CRAZIEST INVENTIONS!

IN MANY RELIGIONS, THE VIRGIN IS WORSHIPPED AS THE MOST VALUED FEMALE FIGURE.

HERE YOU GO—72 VIRGINS. WELL DESERVED!

IN ANCIENT ROME, SELECTED VIRGINS FROM ESTEEMED FAMILIES WERE CHOSEN TO BE "VESTALS."

CONGRATS!

WELCOME TO THE TEMPLE OF VESTA! HERE YOU WILL TEND THE SACRED FIRE.

A VESTAL WHO BROKE HER PROMISE TO REMAIN A VIRGIN WAS SEVERELY PUNISHED.

IF YOU SLEEP AROUND, WE WILL LOCK YOU UP...

SINCE THE VESTAL WAS HOLY, NO ROMAN WOULD LAY A HAND ON HER; THEREFORE, SHE WAS BURIED ALIVE.

FOREVER...

SEXUALLY ACTIVE WOMEN HAVE ALWAYS BEEN DISCRIMINATED AGAINST.

KILL ALL THE BOYS, AND ALL THE WOMEN WHO HAVE LAIN WITH MEN!

MOSES IS IRRITATED WITH THE SOLDIERS BECAUSE THEY HAVEN'T KILLED THE ENEMY'S WOMEN:

BUT LET ALL THE YOUNG GIRLS WHO HAVE NOT LAIN WITH MEN LIVE!

WHORE!

STRUMPET!

SLUT!

HARLOT!

HUSSY!

IN THE 1800S, IT WAS WIDELY BELIEVED THAT WOMEN HAD NO SEXUAL DESIRES. IF A WOMAN SEEMED INTERESTED IN SEX, MEN WERE HAPPY TO DIAGNOSE HER.

SO WHAT YOU'RE TRYING TO SAY IS YOU *WANT* SEX?

YES, SOMETIMES.

PATIENT RECORD

PATIENT RECORD

NYMPHOMANIAC

ABNORMAL

PATIENT RECORD

PATIENT RECORD

INSANE

PATIENT RECORD

HERMAPHRODITE

HYSTERICAL

SO-CALLED "SLUT-SHAMING" (SHAMING WOMEN FOR THEIR SEXUALITY) IS A WIDESPREAD HISTORICAL PHENOMENON.

LOOSE WOMAN...

TSK, TSK...

THE DAILY NEWS
TEMPTED HIM

THE POST
REGRET
People forgive

SHOCK!!

Woman behind the SEX SCANDAL

10:-

WE FIND EVIDENCE OF THIS RUMORMONGERING IN MANY OLD STORIES:

SEXUALLY PROMISCUOUS

JULIA THE ELDER, BORN 39 BCE

VERY PROMISCUOUS

CLODIA, BORN CA. 94 BCE

PROMISCUOUS AND DOMINEERING

VALERIA MESSALINA, BORN CA. 20 CE

PROMISCUOUS

MARGARET OF VALOIS, BORN 1553

LOOSE WOMAN

ÉMILIE DU CHÂTELET, BORN 1706

PROMISCUOUS

METTE-MARIT, CROWN PRINCESS OF NORWAY, BORN 1973

MARAT WAS A MEMBER OF THE SOCIETY OF THE JACOBINS, WHICH TERRORIZED AND KILLED ITS OPPONENTS. CHARLOTTE CORDAY THOUGHT THAT KILLING ONE MAN WOULD SAVE HUNDREDS OF THOUSANDS.

ALTHOUGH SHE CLAIMED SOLE RESPONSIBILITY FOR THE ASSASSINATION, THE JACOBINS DIDN'T BELIEVE HER.

SHE MUST HAVE BEEN PUT UP TO IT BY A MAN!

CLEARLY!

A GROTESQUE AUTOPSY WAS THEREFORE CONDUCTED, BECAUSE IF CORDAY *WASN'T* A VIRGIN, *THAT* WOULD PROVE SHE HAD A MALE ACCOMPLICE.

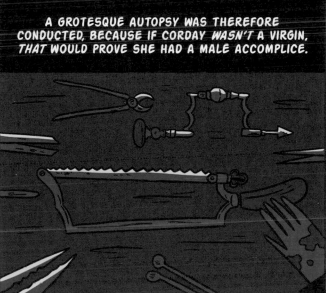

Panel 1:
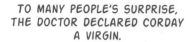
TO MANY PEOPLE'S SURPRISE, THE DOCTOR DECLARED CORDAY A VIRGIN.

DEFINITELY A VIRGIN!

Panel 2:

IT'S NOT ACTUALLY POSSIBLE TO DETERMINE SUCH A THING. THERE IS NO MAIDENHEAD, JUST A FOLD OF SKIN CALLED THE HYMEN.

SHH, THE STORY ISN'T OVER!

THE TERM "MAIDENHEAD" IS NOW OFTEN REPLACED BY THE MORE ACCURATE TERM "HYMEN." WHAT WE HAVE IS AN ELASTIC FOLD OF SKIN THAT CAN STRETCH A LOT WITHOUT CAUSING ANY TEARS OR BLEEDS. THEREFORE, NO INVESTIGATION CAN DETERMINE WHETHER YOU HAVE HAD SEX OR NOT.

Panel 3:

THE AUTHORITIES WERE WORRIED ABOUT CORDAY'S LEGACY: THE BEAUTIFUL VIRGINAL MARTYR WHO WANTED TO SAVE HER COUNTRY.

SHE SOUNDS LIKE A NEW JOAN OF ARC.

SOMETHING MUST BE DONE!

Panel 4:
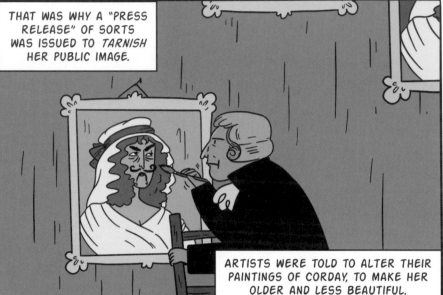
THAT WAS WHY A "PRESS RELEASE" OF SORTS WAS ISSUED TO *TARNISH* HER PUBLIC IMAGE.

ARTISTS WERE TOLD TO ALTER THEIR PAINTINGS OF CORDAY, TO MAKE HER OLDER AND LESS BEAUTIFUL.

Panel 5:

UNFORTUNATELY, CHARLOTTE CORDAY'S ACT WAS SOON USED AS AN ARGUMENT AGAINST WOMEN'S SUFFRAGE.

NOW WE HAVE PROOF! POLITICS IS NO PLACE FOR WOMEN!

BAN WOMEN'S SALONS!

Panel 6:

AND BEHEAD THAT OLYMPE DE GOUGES*, TOO!

!?!

*OLYMPE DE GOUGES WAS A FRENCH WRITER AND FEMINIST WHO WAS GUILLOTINED IN 1793.

58

AT THE SAME TIME IN LONDON:
THE SLUT-SHAMING OF MARY WOLLSTONECRAFT
BRITISH PHILOSOPHER AND AUTHOR MARY WOLLSTONECRAFT WAS PART OF A RADICAL LITERARY SCENE IN LONDON AT THE END OF THE 1700S.
LIBERTÉ, ÉGALITÉ, FRATERNITÉ !!
MARY WOLLSTONECRAFT
WILLIAM GODWIN
JOSEPH JOHNSON
HENRY FUSELI
THOMAS PAINE
J. Johnson Publishing

WHEN MARY WAS A CHILD, SCHOOL WAS ONLY FOR THE RICH—AND BOYS WERE PRIORITIZED OVER GIRLS.

YOUNG MIDDLE-CLASS GIRLS WERE EXPECTED TO WAIT FOR A MARRIAGE PROPOSAL...

AND THEN LET THEIR HUSBAND PROVIDE FOR THEM.

BUT WHEN MARY WAS ONLY 15, SHE DECLARED:

AFTER STINTS AS A GOVERNESS, LADY'S COMPANION, AND TEACHER, MARY WOLLSTONECRAFT DECIDED TO BECOME AN AUTHOR.

AT THAT TIME, VERY FEW WOMEN WROTE UNDER THEIR OWN NAMES.

WOLLSTONECRAFT HAD HER BIG BREAKTHROUGH AS AN AUTHOR IN 1792 WITH THE BOOK *A VINDICATION OF THE RIGHTS OF WOMAN.*

SHE TOOK ISSUE WITH FRENCH PHILOSOPHER JEAN-JACQUES ROUSSEAU, WHO SAID GIRLS SHOULD BE RAISED TO PLEASE MEN.

WOMEN ARE JUST AS SMART AS MEN.

A VINDICATION OF THE RIGHTS OF WOMAN ... MARY WOLLSTONECRAFT

MANY WOMEN ARE MORE INTERESTED IN BEAUTY AND EMBROIDERY THAN SCIENCE AND POLITICS BECAUSE THEY'RE BROUGHT UP THAT WAY.

IF GIRLS AND BOYS RECEIVED THE SAME SCHOOLING, THAT WOULD CHANGE.

THE BOOK WAS DEEMED A SCANDAL, AND MARY BECAME FAMOUS OVERNIGHT.

PUBLIC DEBATES WERE ARRANGED WHERE THE BOOK—AND THE AUTHOR— WERE DISCUSSED AT LENGTH.

SHE'S VERY MASCULINE!

EMOTIONALLY UNSTABLE!

ALMOST SEXLESS, I'D SAY.

A HYENA IN A PETTICOAT!

THE FRENCH REVOLUTION MADE A BIG IMPRESSION ON MARY WOLLSTONECRAFT.

IN HER PAMPHLETS, SHE RAGED AGAINST THE ARISTOCRACY AND FOR DEMOCRACY.

IN DECEMBER 1792, SHE TRAVELED TO FRANCE TO STUDY THE REVOLUTION UP CLOSE.

PARIS WAS IN CHAOS, AND VIOLENCE WAS INCREASING.

MARY WROTE A NEW BOOK WHERE SHE CONFRONTED THE VIOLENT CULTURE.

WHEN VISITING SOME BRITISH FRIENDS IN PARIS, SHE MET AN AMERICAN CAPTAIN, GILBERT IMLAY.

THEY FELL IN LOVE AND MOVED TO THE CITY OF LE HAVRE IN NORTHERN FRANCE...

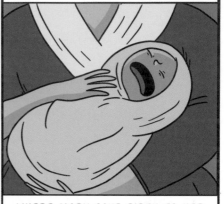

WHERE MARY GAVE BIRTH TO HER FIRST CHILD, FANNY.

IT SOON BECAME CLEAR THAT GILBERT IMLAY WASN'T INTERESTED IN FAMILY LIFE.

HE REGULARLY TRAVELED AND MET OTHER WOMEN.

MARY WOLLSTONECRAFT LEFT FRANCE AND MOVED BACK TO LONDON.

HEARTBROKEN, SHE WROTE A LETTER TO IMLAY:

I shall plunge into the Thames where there is the least chance of my being snatched from the death I seek.

God bless you! May you never know by experience what you have made me endure.

Should your sensibility ever awake, remorse will find its way to your heart

I HAVE ONLY TO LAMENT THAT, WHEN THE BITTERNESS OF DEATH WAS PAST, I WAS INHUMANELY BROUGHT BACK TO LIFE AND MISERY.

IN 1796, SHE STARTED A RELATIONSHIP WITH RADICAL PHILOSOPHER WILLIAM GODWIN.

I'VE READ YOUR BOOKS, MARY. YOU'RE A GENIUS!

THE FOLLOWING YEAR SHE FELL PREGNANT AGAIN.

BOTH WOLLSTONECRAFT AND GODWIN WERE PRINCIPLED OPPONENTS OF MARRIAGE, BUT THEY NEVERTHELESS DECIDED TO MARRY FOR THE SAKE OF THEIR UNBORN CHILD.

THE COUPLE MOVED INTO A HOUSE CALLED THE POLYGON.

THE HOUSE CONSISTED OF TWO APARTMENTS, SO THEY COULD LIVE APART AND MAINTAIN THEIR INDEPENDENCE.

THEY OFTEN COMMUNICATED BY LETTER.

UNFORTUNATELY, THIS ARRANGEMENT DIDN'T LAST LONG.

DURING THE BIRTH OF HER SECOND DAUGHTER, WOLLSTONECRAFT EXPERIENCE COMPLICATIONS: THE PLACENTA RUPTURED AND BECAME INFECTED.

AFTER FIGHTING FOR SEVERAL DAYS, MARY WOLLSTONECRAFT DIED OF BLOOD POISONING AT THE AGE OF 38.

HER DAUGHTER SURVIVED AND WAS NAMED MARY, AFTER HER MOTHER.

MARY SHELLEY, THE AUTHOR OF *FRANKENSTEIN*

MARY WOLLSTONECRAFT
1759-1797

WILLIAM GODWIN WAS GRIEF-STRICKEN.

I firmly believe there does not exist her equal in the world. I have not the least expectation that I can ever know happiness again.

MEMOIRS OF THE AUTHOR OF A VINDICATION OF THE RIGHTS OF WOMAN

THREE YEARS LATER, HE HAD HIS WIFE'S MEMOIRS PUBLISHED.

THE WIDOWER INTENDED THE BOOK TO BE A LOVING PORTRAIT, BUT READERS WERE SHOCKED BY THE PRIVATE REVELATIONS.

MARY WAS THEREFORE THE SUBJECT OF EVEN MORE SCANDAL AFTER HER DEATH.

SHE HAD CHILDREN OUT OF WEDLOCK?

SUICIDE ATTEMPTS? THAT'S JUST AWFUL!

AUTHORS AND POETS WROTE SCORNFUL COMPOSITIONS AND SARCASTIC NOVELS ABOUT HER.

MARY WOLLSTONECRAFT'S REPUTATION WAS IN TATTERS THROUGHOUT THE 1800S.

IN TIME, HER BOOKS WERE DISCOVERED BY A NEW WOMEN'S MOVEMENT.

SHE INFLUENCED PIONEERS SUCH AS LUCRETIA MOTT, ELIZABETH CADY STANTON, EMMA GOLDMAN, AND MILLICENT FAWCETT.

IT COULD BE ARGUED THAT SHE WAS THE GODMOTHER OF THE FIRST WAVE OF FEMINISM.

MORE THAN 100 YEARS AFTER MARY WOLLSTONECRAFT AND CHARLOTTE CORDAY WERE INVOLVED IN THE FRENCH REVOLUTION CAME THE RUSSIAN REVOLUTION.

UNION OF WOMEN WORKERS

Peace now!

Peace!!

ONE OF THE LEADING FIGURES THERE WAS ALEXANDRA KOLLONTAI (1872–1952).

KOLLONTAI MARRIED WHEN SHE WAS 20 BUT LEFT HER FAMILY TO STUDY SOCIAL ECONOMICS IN SWITZERLAND...

WHERE SHE MET WOMEN'S RIGHTS ADVOCATE CLARA ZETKIN. THEY STARTED WORKING TOGETHER.

ALEXANDRA KOLLONTAI WAS A CLOSE ASSOCIATE OF VLADIMIR LENIN, AND AFTER THE OCTOBER REVOLUTION IN 1917, SHE WAS APPOINTED PEOPLE'S COMMISSAR FOR SOCIAL WELFARE.

SHE INTRODUCED A NUMBER OF RADICAL REFORMS:

EQUAL PAY FOR EQUAL WORK.

WOMEN WERE GIVEN MATERNITY LEAVE AND PAID BREASTFEEDING BREAKS.

IT BECAME EASIER TO FILE FOR DIVORCE AND TO HAVE AN ABORTION.

KOLLONTAI CAMPAIGNED FOR FREE LOVE AND WOMEN'S SEXUAL LIBERATION.

MARRIAGE SHOULD BE ABOLISHED!

SHE WAS PARTICULARLY INTERESTED IN COLLECTIVISM.

HER DREAM WAS TO TRANSFER THE RESPONSIBILITY FOR HOUSEWORK AND CHILDREARING FROM INDIVIDUAL WOMEN TO THE COMMUNITY.

THIS MESSAGE SCARED MANY CONSERVATIVE RUSSIANS, WHO ACCUSED HER OF CORRUPTING YOUNG PEOPLE.

HER COMMUNIST FRIENDS SOON TURNED AGAINST HER, TOO.

AT THE 1921 CONGRESS OF THE COMINTERN, SHE WAS SLUT-SHAMED BY BOTH LENIN AND LEON TROTSKY.

AMAZON!

VALKYRIE!

WHEN JOSEF STALIN CAME INTO POWER, HE IMMEDIATELY SCRAPPED ALL THE NEW REFORMS.

ALEXANDRA KOLLONTAI WAS ONE OF THE FEW BOLSHEVIKS TO SURVIVE STALIN'S REGIME.

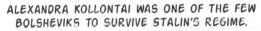

AMBASSADØR

SHE LIVED IN EXILE IN NORWAY AND SWEDEN FOR A LONG TIME, AND WAS APPOINTED THE WORLD'S FIRST FEMALE AMBASSADOR.

A *UNIVERSAL GENIUS, EVEN!*

PHILOSOPHER

POET

POLITICIAN

SCIENTIST

ACCORDING TO WIKIPEDIA, A GENIUS IS A PERSON WHO DISPLAYS EXCEPTIONAL INTELLECTUAL ABILITY, ORIGINALITY, AND CREATIVE PRODUCTIVITY ACROSS MANY SUBJECTS.

THE WORD GENIUS COMES FROM LATIN, AND IN THE ROMAN RELIGION IT DESCRIBED A *MAN'S* CHARACTERISTIC DISPOSITION.

PATER FAMILIAS

GOETHE EXHIBITED SIGNS OF GENIUS AS A BOY.

BARBA TENUS SAPIENTES!

HE WROTE HIS FIRST POEMS AT THE AGE OF SEVEN, AND BY NINE HAD MASTERED GREEK, LATIN, THE PIANO, AND FENCING.

THE FAMILY HAD THREE SERVANTS, CLEANERS, A COOK, AND THEIR OWN WIGMAKER.

AS A YOUNG MAN, GOETHE STARTED STUDYING LAW.

SIGH...

BUT REALLY, HE WAS MORE INTERESTED IN LITERATURE...

SIGH...

AND WOMEN.

HE SOON BECAME PART OF THE YOUTH ARTS MOVEMENT "STURM UND DRANG."

THE MOVEMENT WAS EXACTLY THE OPPOSITE OF THE COLD, COMMON-SENSE APPROACH THAT PREVAILED DURING THE ENLIGHTENMENT, WHICH WAS ALSO KNOWN AS THE AGE OF REASON.

STURM UND DRANG WRITERS WERE MORE INTERESTED IN EMOTION, NATURE, AND ROMANCE.

GOETHE HIMSELF WROTE THE MOST IMPORTANT BOOK OF THE ERA:

THE SORROWS OF YOUNG WERTHER

JOHANN WOLFGANG VON GOETHE

IT TELLS THE STORY OF A PASSIONATE BOY, WERTHER, WHO FALLS IN LOVE WITH A GIRL CALLED LOTTE.

UNFORTUNATELY, SHE IS IN LOVE WITH ALBERT.

HELLO, FRIENDS!

WERTHER HANGS AROUND ALBERT AND LOTTE FOR A LONG TIME.

ISN'T THIS NICE?

UNTIL THEY'VE HAD ENOUGH OF HIM.

THEN HE TAKES HIS OWN LIFE.

THE BOOK WAS A CULT PHENOMENON, BUT UNFORTUNATELY MANY YOUNG PEOPLE TOOK THE CONTENT TOO LITERALLY.

THEY STARTED TO DRESS LIKE WERTHER...

OH, THIS EMPTINESS! THIS TERRIBLE EMPTINESS THAT DWELLS IN MY BREAST!

TALK LIKE WERTHER...

AND END IT ALL, LIKE WERTHER.

HISTORIANS ESTIMATE THAT AROUND 2,000 MEN COMMITTED SUICIDE AFTER READING THE NOVEL.

GOETHE, HOWEVER, BECAME A FAMOUS AND CELEBRATED AUTHOR OVERNIGHT.

BUT HE WAS ALREADY TIRED OF WERTHER AND ROMANCE. NOW HE WANTED TO CONCENTRATE ON HIS LIFE'S GREAT WORK, *FAUST*.

Dr. Faust

Shh! Genius at work!!

GOETHE'S VERSION OF THE OLD GERMAN SAGA TELLS THE STORY OF WANNABE GENIUS JOHANN FAUST.

HIS BIG DREAM IS TO BE OMNISCIENT—TO KNOW EVERYTHING,

TO ACHIEVE THIS, HE AGREES TO SELL HIS SOUL TO THE DEVIL.

USING HIS DIABOLICAL SUPERPOWERS, FAUST TRAVELS AROUND THE WORLD AND DOES GREAT THINGS.

HE ALSO TEMPTS A YOUNG AND CHASTE WOMAN NAMED GRETCHEN.

SHE GOES TO CHURCH, SPINS YARN, AND SINGS BEAUTIFUL SONGS.

LIKE MANY OTHER FEMALE ROLES IN WORLD LITERATURE, GRETCHEN IS MORE OF A SYMBOL THAN AN ACTUAL PERSON.

FAUST KILLS HER BROTHER AND MAKES GRETCHEN KILL THEIR CHILD. SHE GOES INSANE AND IS EXECUTED.

THE PLAY ENDS WITH GOD TAKING PITY ON FAUST, SO THAT MEPHISTOPHELES IS CHEATED OF HIS SOUL.

TODAY, ACTIVISTS IMPRISONED IN COUNTRIES SUCH AS IRAN AND SAUDI ARABIA ARE ACCUSED OF REMOVING THEIR HEADSCARVES OR FIGHTING FOR WOMEN'S RIGHTS IN OTHER WAYS.

FEMINISTS ARE PORTRAYED IN NEWSPAPERS AS HUMORLESS, ANGRY, AND UNATTRACTIVE...

UGH, UGH!

VOTES FOR WOMEN

EW!!

AS FRIGID...

IT'S DEFINITELY THE RIGHT DIAGNOSIS.

DR. EXPERTSEN

AND AS BAD MOTHERS.

RIGHT TO VOTE NOW!!

AND WHERE ARE YOUR CHILDREN TODAY, HM?

THE HISTORY OF MEN'S OPPOSITION TO WOMEN'S EMANCIPATION IS MORE INTERESTING PERHAPS THAN THE STORY OF THAT EMANCIPATION ITSELF.

VIRGINIA WOOLF (1882-1941)

NEVERTHELESS, NEW GENERATIONS OF WOMEN WHO DARE TO CALL THEMSELVES PROUD FEMINISTS CONTINUE TO EMERGE.

#METOO

THIS IS WHAT A FEMINIST LOOKS LIKE

THE INTERNET HAS MADE IT EASIER TO KEEP IN TOUCH ACROSS BORDERS...

AND EASIER TO ARRANGE BIG DEMONSTRATIONS.

SMASH THE PATRIARCHY

WOMEN'S MARCH

WOMEN TODAY ARE HIGHLY EDUCATED...

AND HAVE MORE POWER THAN EVER.

IN MODERN FEMINISM, IT IS COMMON TO DRAW PARALLELS BETWEEN DIFFERENT TYPES OF DISCRIMINATION.
FOR EXAMPLE, IT ISN'T ONLY WOMEN WHO EXPERIENCE BEING BRANDED AS "OTHER."
ANYONE WHO DEFIES SOCIETAL NORMS HAS TO FIGHT FOR THEIR RIGHTS.
MY BODY MY CHOICE!!
THE FUTURE IS INCLUSIVE

ARISTOTLE!!
OF COURSE, NO ONE DOES IT BETTER.
THANK YOU!
CONGRATULATIONS!
1
2
3
Worst Sexist

Honorable Mentions

Donald Trump
Ayatollah Khomeini
Jeffrey Epstein
Pablo Picasso
Silvio Berlusconi

Jair Bolsonaro
Viktor Orbán
Vladimir Putin
Heinrich Heine
Dominique Strauss-Kahn
R. Kelly
Jack Kerouac
Recep Tayyip Erdogan
Harvey Weinstein
Bill Cosby
Ingmar Bergman
Confucius
Hugh Hefner
Norman Mailer
Richard Polwhele
Aleksandr Lukashenko
Jarosław Kaczynski
Todd Akin

Jordan Peterson
Gustav Vigeland
Saul Bellow
Knut Hamsun
Johan Christian Heuch
Roman Polanski
Rush Limbaugh
Björn Afzelius

Ole Olsen Malm
John Wayne
Axel Jensen
Carl David af Wirsén
Terry Richardson
Larry Flynt
Otto Weininger
William Acton
Thomas Aquinas
William S. Burroughs
Theodor Von Bischoff
Nicolas Restif De
La Bretonne
Gustav Mahler
Pierre-Auguste Renoir
Augustin
Charles Darwin
Martin Luther
August Strindberg
Sigmund Freud
Albert Einstein
Napoleon Bonaparte
Gautama Buddha

Ayn Rand
Charles Baudelaire
Lars Von Trier
Thommy Berggren
Jørgen Leth
Piers Morgan
John Paul Getty
Ludvig Nessa

Steve Bannon
Joe Scheidler
Frank Pavone
Stewart Allen-Clark
Julien Blanc
Elvis Presley
J. D. Salinger
Göran Lambertz

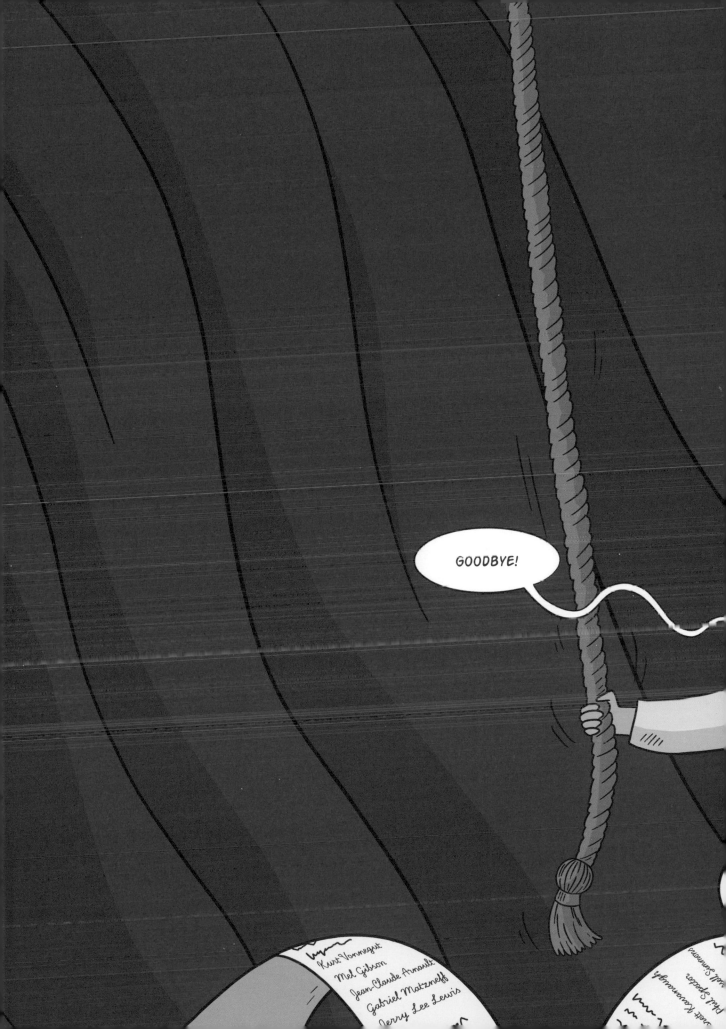